GRANDFATHER, I WANT TO HEAR YOUR STORY

Created by Romney Nelson

A Place to Share My Life Memories. Grandfather xx

"Of all the titles I've been privileged to have,

'Dad' has always been the best."

- Ken Norton -

THE BEGINNING...

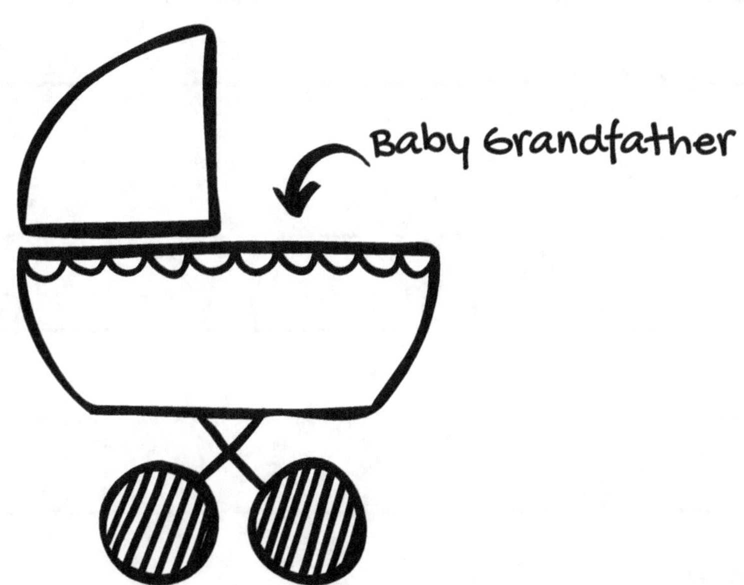

MY INTRODUCTION

Before I start....just a brief introduction about me!

Name:

Signature

Date

THE BEGINNING......

Full Name at Birth

Date of Birth / /

Time of Birth :

Day of the week you were born?

Height at birth? (if known)

Weight at birth? (If known)

Your Place of Birth (include the City/Town, Country)

Did you have any siblings when you were born? If so, what were their names and their ages?

ADD ANY ADDITIONAL NOTES OR INFORMATION HERE...

THE BEGINNING......

Share with us some information about your parents?

Were you in good health as a baby?

Did you have any unique characteristics or funny things you did as a baby?

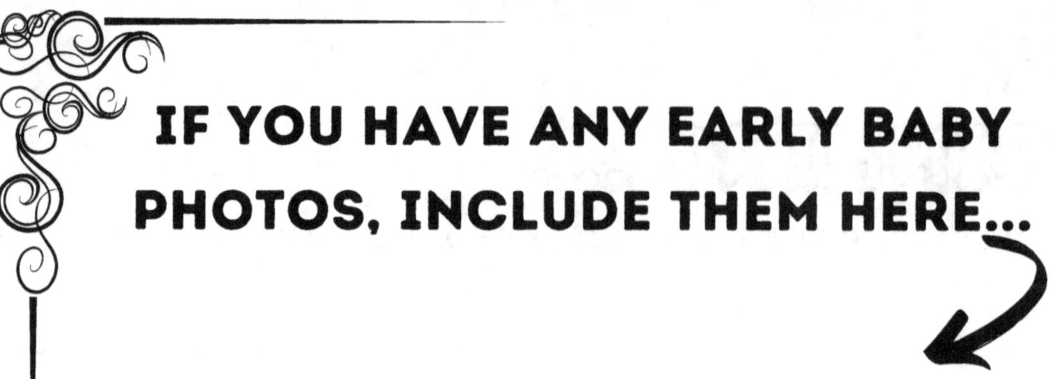
IF YOU HAVE ANY EARLY BABY
PHOTOS, INCLUDE THEM HERE...

THE BEGINNING……

Were you an active or quiet baby?

Were you ever told what your first words were?

Do you have any other baby memories to share?

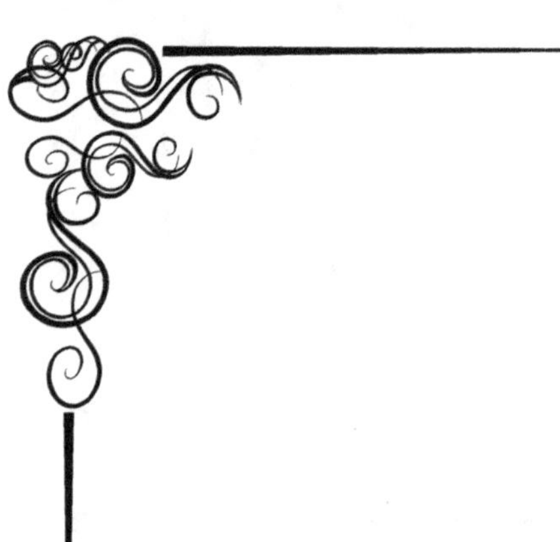

"Every father should remember one day his son or daughter will follow his example, not his advice."

— Charles Kettering -

FAMILY HISTORY

FAMILY HISTORY

My grandparents names were:

Grandmother: ____________________

Grandfather: ____________________

They were born in: (country)
Grandmother: ____________________

Grandfather: ____________________

This is something that not many people may know about our family history......

____

____

____

____

____

Additional Family History information:

____

____

____

Our FAMILY TREE

GrandFather

GrandFather

Grandmother

Grandmother

Mother

Father

Me

ADD ANY ADDITIONAL NOTES OR INFORMATION HERE...

CHILDHOOD YEARS

CHILDHOOD YEARS....

What was your favorite toy growing up?

Did you have a pet or any pets growing up?

What was your favorite T.V show to watch as a child?

Was there a moment you remember getting into big trouble as a child? Was there a punishment?

ADD ANY ADDITIONAL NOTES OR INFORMATION HERE...

CHILDHOOD YEARS....

What are your fondest memories growing up between the ages of 5 - 12 years?

IF YOU HAVE ANY EARLY CHILDHOOD
PHOTOS, PLACE THEM HERE...

CHILDHOOD YEARS....

Where did you grow up as a child?
(house, location, town etc)

Who was your best friend or your best friends as a child?

What was your favorite day of the week and why?

CHILDHOOD YEARS....

What was your favorite meal as a child?

What elementary/primary school did you attend and where was it located?

Describe your most memorable moment or story from elementary/primary school.

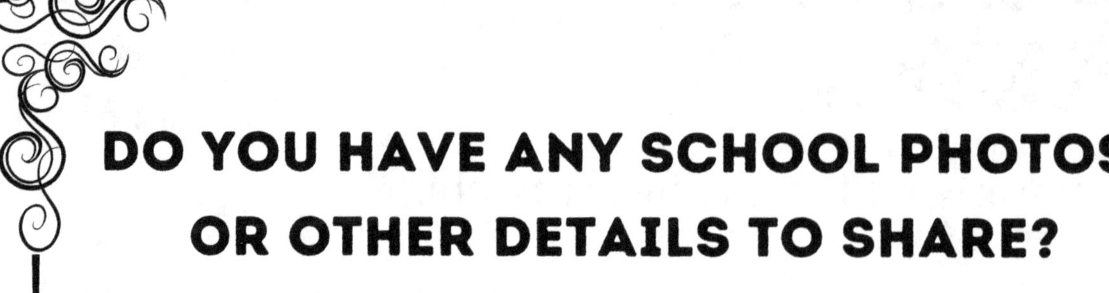

DO YOU HAVE ANY SCHOOL PHOTOS, OR OTHER DETAILS TO SHARE?

TEENAGE YEARS

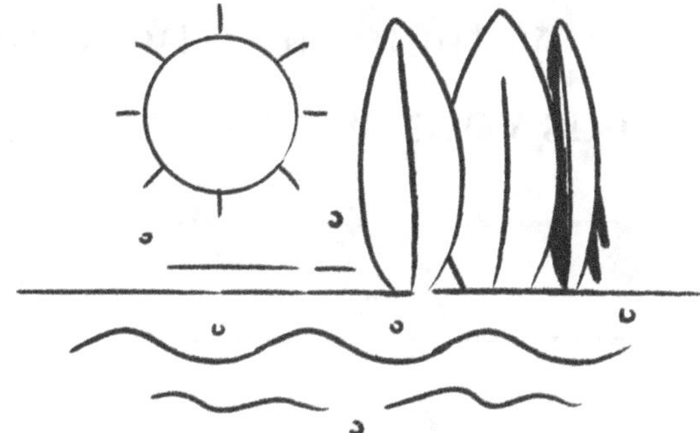

TEENAGE YEARS....

Describe your dress sense and clothing as a teenager. Is there anything that stands out for you?

When and where did you learn to drive a vehicle?

What was your first vehicle and how much did you purchase it for? Tell us your special 'first car' story!

INCLUE ANY 'FIRST VEHICLE' PHOTOS OR OTHER INFORMATION HERE..

TEENAGE YEARS....

What High School did you attend and where was it located?

Who was you favorite teacher or coach and why?

What was your favorite subject at school?

Did you date anyone at High School?

SHARE ANY FURTHER DETAILS HERE

TEENAGE YEARS....

What hobbies did you have as a teenager?

What is your most memorable moment as a teenager?

If you knew what you know today, what would you have done differently as a teenager?

SHARE ANY OTHER DETAILS OR MEMORIES HERE

TEENAGE YEARS....

Did you have a close friendship group? Have you maintained contact with any of them?

Did you have any nicknames at High School?

What 5 words come to mind to describe your teenage years?

1.

2.

3.

4.

5.

WHEN I WAS..

WHEN I WAS....

When I was a child, my mode of transport to school was..

When I was in my teens, the biggest news story that I recall was .....

When I was growing up, my 3 favorite movies were:

1.

2.

3.

WHEN I WAS....

When I was a child, the first movie I went to the theatre to see was..

____

When I graduated from elementary/primary school, the year was.. ______________

When I was a child, I wanted to be a......

____

When I was 18 years old, my favorite music and band was..

____

When I was in my teens, the most popular thing to do on a Saturday night was.......

____

____

When I was young, I loved to travel to.......

____

____

____

____

SHARE ANY FURTHER TRAVEL MEMORIES HERE..

PARENTHOOD

PARENTHOOD....

How old were you when you first became a parent?

Explain how you felt emotionally when you became a parent for the first time?

Where were you located (city/town/country) when you had your first child?

SHARE SOME PARENTING PHOTOS HERE..

PARENTHOOD....

What has been the biggest challenge for you as a parent?

What are 3 key responsibilities you believe are important as a parent?

1

2

3

PARENTHOOD....

EXPAND ON ANY FURTHER PARENTING MEMORIES YOU MAY LIKE TO SHARE

"The quality of a father can be seen in the goals, dreams and aspirations he sets not only for himself, but for his family."

— Reed Markham

MORE ABOUT ME!

MORE ABOUT ME....

Not many people know this about me, so let me share it with you:

The activity or hobby that I enjoy most to do now is.....

I have the unique ability to be able to....

MORE ABOUT ME....

If I was able to go back to a special time in history, it would be...

If I could pass on one word of advice to others, it would be..

There are special moments in life that you wish you could pause to enjoy for longer. Mine would be......

MORE ABOUT ME....

I wish I had the opportunity to...

The quote that resonates most with me is..

My favorite book of all time is:

If there is one thing I would like to be remembered for it would be:

MORE ABOUT ME....

When I look back on my life so far, my 3 proudest moments are:

1 ______________________________

2 ______________________________

3 ______________________________

If there were 3 famous people that I could invite for dinner they would be:

1 ______________________________

2 ______________________________

3 ______________________________

MORE ABOUT ME....

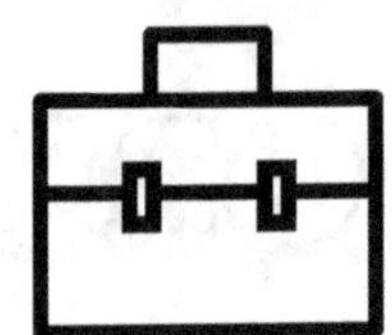

From my teen years, these are the jobs that I've had:

MORE ABOUT ME....

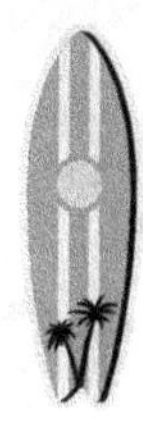

One of the jobs that stands out as my most enjoyable has been..

The most interesting place I have ever traveled to has been.... (include the year/date this occurred)

If I was given a free return flight to anywhere in the world, I would visit...(include your 'Why')

SOME EXTRA SPACE FOR INFORMATION OR PHOTOS HERE..

FINAL NOTES

FINAL NOTES....

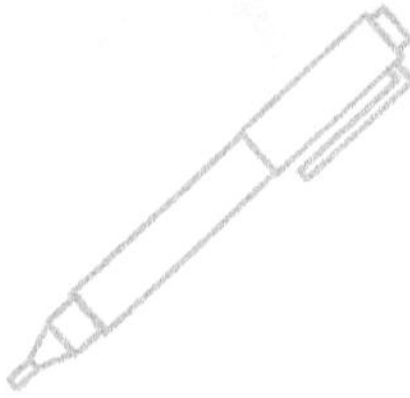

There have been many questions that I have answered in this book, but I would also like to share this with you...

Your time to write anything else you wish to share...

FINAL NOTES....

FINAL NOTES....

FINAL NOTES....

USE THE FOLLOWING PAGES FOR CERTIFICATES, AWARDS. PHOTO'S ETC..

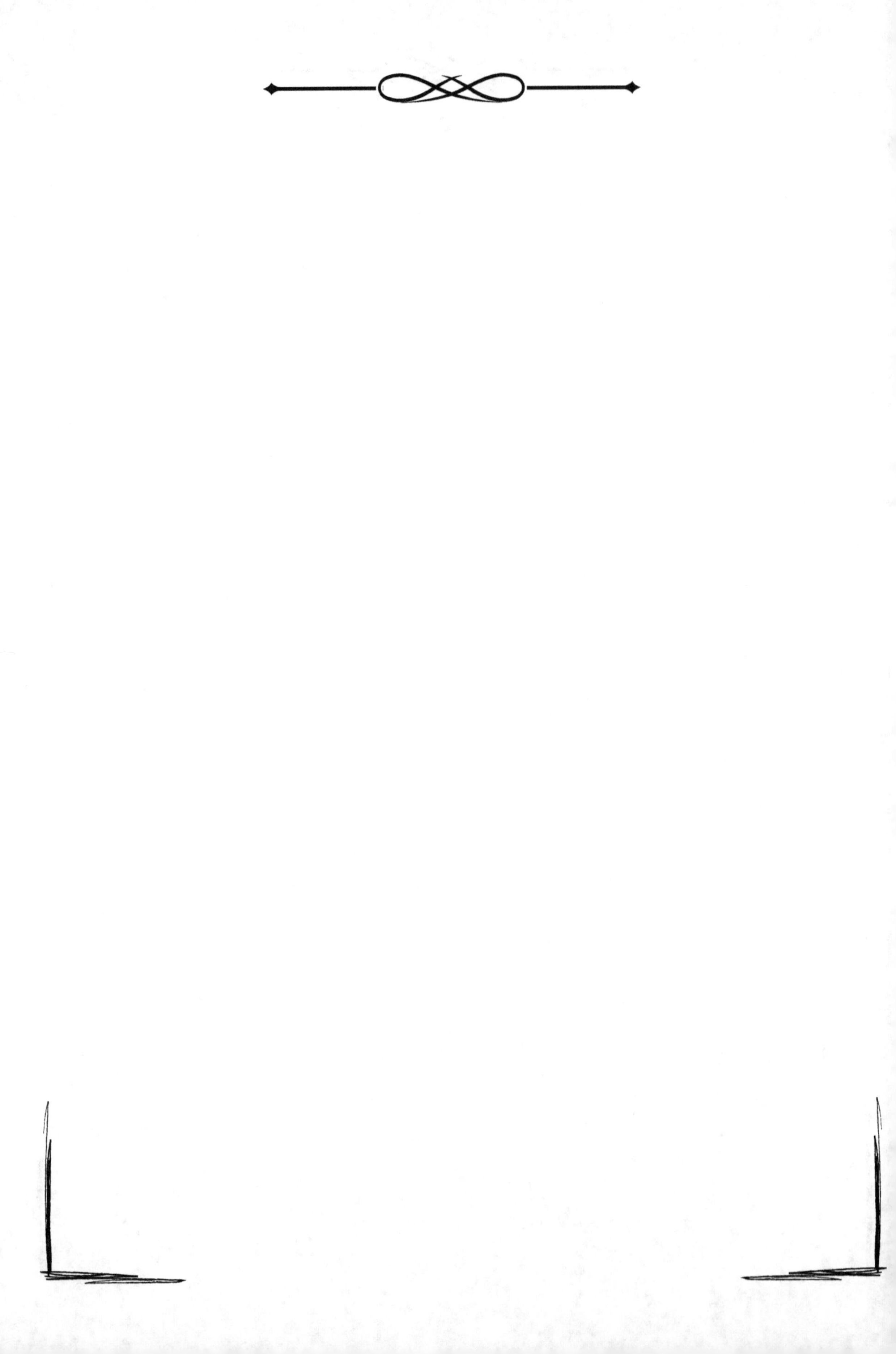

THANK YOU FOR SHARING YOUR LIFE STORY

This book was created by

Romney Nelson

OTHER BOOKS

By

The Life Graduate Publishing Group

www.ingramcontent.com/pod-product-compliance
Lightning Source LLC
Chambersburg PA
CBHW080352030726
47598CB00009B/2717

* 9 7 8 1 9 2 2 4 8 5 9 7 7 *